KILLER BEES

by

Melinda Blau

A
cpi
Book

RSVP
**RAINTREE
STECK-VAUGHN**
PUBLISHERS
The Steck-Vaughn Company

Austin, Texas

First Steck-Vaughn Edition 1992

Art and Photo Credits

Cover illustration by Lynn Sweat.
Illustrations on pages 6, 8, 22, and 43, Connie Maltese.
Photos on page 10, 11, and 40, Ed Zuckerman.
Photo on page 15, Photo Researchers.
Photos on pages 17, 32, and 37, Stephen Dalton/Photo Researchers.
Photo on page 25, R.C. Hermes/Photo Researchers.
Photo on page 27, Colin G. Butler/Photo Researchers.
Photo on page 31, L. West/Photo Researchers.
Photo on page 39, Jane Burton/Bruce Coleman, Inc.
Photo on page 45, Dr. E.R. Degginger/Bruce Coleman, Inc.
Photo on page 47, Russ Kinne/Photo Researchers.
All photo research for this book was provided by Sherry Olan and Roberta Guerrette.
Every effort has been made to trace the ownership of all copyrighted material in this book and to obtain permission for its use.

Library of Congress Number: 77-10010

Library of Congress Cataloging in Publication Data

Blau, Melinda E. 1943-
  Killer Bees.

  SUMMARY: The story of a special strain of honeybees developed by man to increase honey production, but which also has a fierce, belligerent, attacking instinct.
  1. Brazilian honeybee—Juvenile literature. I. Title.
QL568.A6B57   595.7'99   77-10010

ISBN 0-8172-1055-5 hardcover library binding

ISBN 0-8114-6857-7 softcover binding

22 23 24 25 26 WZ 03 02 01 00 99

CONTENTS

VICIOUS ATTACKERS

Señora Massucheto was sitting inside her hut when it happened. She couldn't believe her eyes. Outside, a huge swarm of bees was viciously attacking two horses and a small dog. The dog, covered with bee stings, howled in pain. Señora Massucheto's husband, a Brazilian farmer, rushed to help the family pet. *That was her husband's fatal mistake.*

The bees turned from the dog to the 65-year-old farmer. Within seconds, his body was covered with buzzing insects. Señora Massucheto ran outside and cried out to her husband, "Escape!" But all he could do was cry.

In moments the bees had covered both the man and his dog.

He saved his dog, but the poor farmer died
from the hundreds of stings about his body.
The horses died too. "There were more bees

than hair on them," Señora Massucheto later recalled.

Officials in Curitiba, Brazil, where the Massuchetos lived, wanted to learn more about the farmer's horrible death. When the body was examined, they discovered that the angry bees had flown inside the poor man's mouth and down his throat! More than 80 bees were found in the farmer's stomach!

In 1965, two years after the farmer's death, Dr. Eglantina Portugal was walking to work in a Brazilian city. She was a teacher. Just as she arrived at school a bee stung her. She slapped the insect, killing it. Suddenly, thousands of bees appeared out of nowhere. It was as if the insects knew that one of their own kind had been killed. They seemed to want revenge. *They got it!*

Dr. Eglantina ran, but it was too late. She tripped and fell into a ditch. She crawled out, but her body was covered with bees, and more were on the way. What was worse, no one could help her.

A person sitting in a car near the scene of the attack remembered, "I wanted to help, but it was impossible to leave my closed car. There were bees all over it."

Others tried to rescue Dr. Eglantina by pouring water on the bees. It didn't work. The rescuers, too, were stung. Police who arrived on the scene were also swarmed by the bees. Local firemen were called to join the rescue. They were powerless at first. High pressure water

Could it possibly be revenge that caused the bees to attack Dr. Eglantina?

hoses did no good at all. Finally, the firemen used smoking torches to chase the bees away. The torches worked. But it was too late for Dr. Eglantina. She was dead, her body covered, head to foot, with angry red stings.

These were only two, among several, "bee attacks" on animals and people in South America. At first, little attention was paid to the scattered reports about some "angry bees on the loose." But by 1976, a writer and photographers from the staff of *National Geographic* magazine were sent to South America to investigate the bees. Word of the bees was spreading throughout the world. By now the bee attacks were so vicious the insects were called *killer bees.*

The magazine team of two men and a woman were guarded by a professional beekeeper. Together, they traveled into the Brazilian bush—a dense tropical area near the city of Belém. All wore heavy canvas bee suits and veiled hoods. When they reached the bush country, the investigators found more than they had expected. The mystery of the "killer bees" became quite real. *They were now a part of it!*

"The bees came on us like a squall," the writer recalled. "As we drew closer to their

In March, 1977, an expedition led by Ed Zuckerman (left) went to French Guiana to track down killer bees.

hives . . . the torrent broke. The buzzing of countless wings filled the air. . . . Inches from my eyes, frenzied bees clung to my veil and pumped their [barbs] at me through the netting.

So many bees attacked the camera that she [the photographer] could not press a shutter release without squashing some. [The guide] fled as bees stung through his suit. I felt a stinger

A swarm crawls over a man's arm after being cut down from a tree, branch and all, on the Zuckerman expedition.

pierce my glove and had to fight my own urge to run."

Protected by their canvas suits, the magazine investigators lived to tell the world their story. They even brought back pictures to show those who doubted their story. The investigators were much luckier than many Brazilians. According to reports, over 150 of them have been killed by these bees during the last 10 years. Even more frightening—the bees now seem to be on the march. They are moving north, towards Mexico and the United States at a rate of about 200 miles a year.

Where do the "killer bees" come from? How can they be stopped? What makes them so vicious? *Where will they move next?*

Chapter 2

AN ACCIDENT OF BIRTH?

Interestingly enough, the killer bees were created, not by nature, but by *humans*. It all began in 1956. The Brazilian government asked Dr. Warwick E. Kerr to try to improve Brazil's honey production. Kerr was a *geneticist*—a scientist who develops new breeds of living things by mating one type with another. Dr. Kerr's specialty was breeding insects.

At the time Dr. Kerr began his work at the University in São Paulo, only European honeybees were found in Brazil. Dr. Kerr decided to mate these bees with honeybees from Africa. The African bees were fierce and aggressive but widely known for the large amount of honey they produced. The European bees were known for their gentle personalities. By cross-mating the two, Kerr thought he could produce the perfect honeybee. His bees would be gentle, and they would be good honey producers. *At least, that's what he thought he would get!*

He imported 35 African bees and placed them in an isolated hive. He had to keep these bees separated from the others. Kerr knew the African bees were very dangerous to humans. Most bees do not attack unless they are in danger. But the African bees were known to attack often without cause.

Dr. Kerr covered the hives in such a way that only the worker bees could go in or out. The worker bees were safe to let out of the hive because they are laborers only—they don't mate with other bees.

But Kerr knew that the larger queen bees had to be kept trapped inside the hive. The queens do mate. If they got away, they could start whole new colonies of fierce, highly vicious

In this hive the bees are able to come and go at will.

bees that might attack animals and even humans, without cause.

For a time, Dr. Kerr's experiment went as planned. He slowly allowed the African and European bees to mate in small numbers. His

new breed—part European, part African—
worked much harder than the European bees.
They awakened two hours earlier and stayed on
the job later in the evening. They also hunted
for food at lower temperatures than their
European cousins. They even worked in the
rain! As a result, the new breed of Africanized
bees produced more honey—twice as much as
the original Brazilian bees.

At first, Dr. Kerr was thrilled with the results of cross-breeding the two types of bees.
The African bees influenced the new breed's
honey production. Then came one part of the experiment Dr. Kerr did not expect. When he
started, he believed the gentle European bee
would calm the African bee's personality. *There,
he was wrong.* Very wrong. The new bee in-
herited *both* traits from the Africans. It was defi-
nitely making more honey, but it was also more
vicious. Dr. Kerr had created a small, hard-
working monster—the *killer bee*.

His error soon became obvious to Dr. Kerr
and his beekeepers. Luckily, the new bees were
still captives, kept far away from their gentler
cousins. Dr. Kerr immediately tried to correct
his mistake. The idea was to keep cross-breeding

The eyes of these bee pupae are clearly visible
well before they hatch.

the bees until a hard-working, gentle insect could be produced. He was about to create this new breed of bee when something *terrible* happened.

In 1957, a year after Kerr's experiment began with the African bees, a visiting beekeeper mistakenly set free the vicious queen bees. Suddenly, 26 dangerous African bees began their invasion of Brazil. Their invasion has never stopped. In fact, some say this is only the beginning. Each day, more and more African bees are hatching, free to roam the countryside and spread fear and panic among the people.

Chapter 3

BIONIC BEES?

What makes the Africanized bee so dangerous? Is it more intelligent than other honeybees? Probably not. All bees are able to do some amazing things. They can tell one another when their food supply is low. And most bees can keep the hive temperature at a comfortable level. While inside the hive, they can ward off dangers from the outside. If one bee still outside the hive is in danger, it can call for help. Thousands of other bees in the hive are summoned by the bee's "S. O. S." The bee can release an alarm odor called a *pheromone* that acts almost like a siren to other bees.

The new Africanized bee can do all this and more. It seems to be much stronger than other types of bees—sort of a *super* bee. Like its African ancestors, it can fly longer and farther than other bees. The killer bee has flown across the Amazon River and even greater distances!

The Africanized bee is also able to cope with changes in the environment that the European honeybee could not survive. For example, when ordinary honeybees are faced with a food shortage, they huddle in the hive and die. The Africanized "bionic" bees do not give up nearly so easily. They keep moving, going as far as they have to in order to find a new food supply. When the bees are on a long search, a 17-pound hive may weigh less than a pound. But once food is found, the bees return. They start to produce honey again and the hive is back to normal within 90 days! That's an incredible rate of survival.

The killer bees are also more dangerous. In fact, these Africanized super bees are downright *nasty*. Bee experts who have studied killer bees say that these bees are far more fierce than their African ancestors. They fly in greater numbers and stay "on the attack" for longer periods of time. They also will attack just about anything that moves. A Brazilian farmer, plowing his field, was attacked by a few bees. Dozens more quickly joined the attacking few. The farmer was smart enough to jump off his moving tractor and run. Fortunately, the bees followed the moving tractor, instead of him. He is one of the rare killer bee victims who lived to tell his story.

The super bees are also very sensitive to noise. The slightest sound can set them off. A funeral procession, a dog barking, gunfire—all these have led to bee attacks in Brazil. And these bees seem more sensitive to odors. When one bee senses danger or an emergency, thousands of others, responding to its *pheromone,* are sure to follow

One experiment illustrated just how mean these bees can get. When an experimenter dangled a soft, black leather pouch near a hive, the bees were angered to attack. The man who performed the experiment wanted to find out how many times the bees would sting the pouch. He was going to time them every 30 seconds. Once the attack began, the bees became so wild that he thought it best to walk away before the 30 seconds were up. In 5 seconds, the black leather pouch had been stung 92 times!

Even though the experimenter walked away, the bees didn't give up. In fact, they followed him for three-quarters of a mile, as if de-

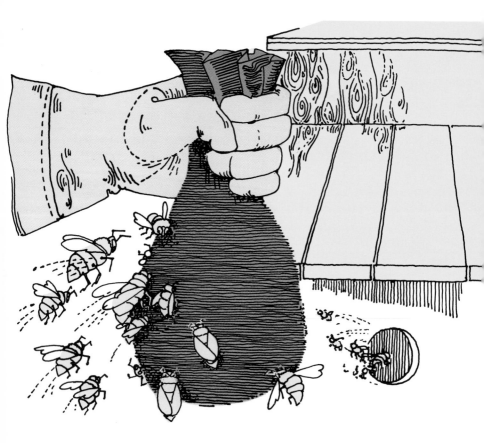

The bees wildly attacked the black leather pouch.

termined to kill him. Once they are angered, these "bionic" bees take a long time to quiet down. While other bees stay upset for only three or four hours at most, killer bees stay angry for a whole day. Not only do they hold a grudge, but their stings are far more deadly!

Scientists were amazed at how quickly the killer bee became the supreme bee in Brazil. By breeding with the European bee, the Africanized bee knocked out the milder types. It might have taken another breed longer, but the new Africanized bees seem to break *all* rules!

Chapter 4

THE FLIGHT OF THE BEES

How did the number of killer bees grow so quickly? They multiplied just as other bees—by *swarming*. Swarming is the flight of great numbers of bees, together with their queen, to start new colonies. This is the beginning of the breeding process. Huge numbers of bees from one hive are involved in mating with bees from other hives, and the result is large numbers of new bee colonies.

Swarming is nature's way of making room in each hive for new generations of bees. It also

Because there was no hollow in the tree, wild bees made their nest on this exposed branch.

guarantees great numbers of new bees born each year. The older generation of bees, led by its queen, leaves the hive in search of a new home. By departing, they make room for a new queen who has come of age in the hive. When the 26 African queens were mistakenly set free from Dr. Kerr's laboratory, they immediately sought new hives where they could breed.

Every good beekeeper knows the warning signs of swarming. At first, there is increased activity inside the hive. Suddenly, the old queen departs, bringing with her about half of the bees in the hive. The queen settles for a while on a branch or a parked car or on a roof top. Meanwhile, several worker scouts are sent out to find a new home for the hive.

The worker scouts report back to the queen by doing a waggle-tail dance. The dance tells the queen and other bees how far the new hive is and exactly how they should fly to get there. Soon a new bee colony is formed.

Back at the old hive, the new queens leave their brood cells—the places where they have grown into adult bees. Although more than one queen can live in a hive, it rarely happens. Usually, the first queen that comes out kills the

A large queen is attended by her court of workers.

others. But if two or more queens emerge at the same time, there's a showdown. It's like an old-fashioned gunfight, except the weapons are the queens' venomous stingers instead of six-shooters. The queens fight until only one queen is left. She is the hive's new leader, and no bee in the hive disputes that fact!

A week or two passes. The new queen goes off for her first mating flight. Several male bees called *drones* fly out after her. Each one is in eager pursuit. The one who reaches her first—usually the strongest and fastest—mates with the queen.

When the escaped African queens bred in the forest, new colonies multiplied at an unbelievable rate. Even when some colonies rejected the foreign queen, she fought her way into the hive anyway.

In an effort to control the spreading plague of killer bees, some Brazilian farmers poisoned their bee colonies if the African visitors were seen around. But this didn't work. The killers had already spread out too far. They were faster and stronger than anyone had expected.

Authorities tried a new plan. They released thousands of gentler male Italian bees around the country. This species was known for its pleasant disposition. If these male bees would fertilize the escaped African queens, bees that came from such matings might be less ferocious.

It was too late. Many of the African queens had already mated and produced male workers who were faster and could fly longer than the Italian bees. The male killer bees beat the European bees to the African queens.

Chapter 5

KILL THEM!

If the Africanized bee poses such a great threat to the world, why don't we destroy them all? Surely, we have chemical sprays that could do this job?

The fact is, we don't kill bees because we need them. Of all insects, bees play the most important role in human life. Every year, professional American beekeepers produce over 240 million pounds of honey and 3 to 5 million pounds of beeswax. More importantly, plants

Note the pollen basket on the leg of this honeybee. The nectar is collected from the flower by the bee's tube-like tongue.

and flowers need bees to survive. There would be no way of poisoning only the killer bees. *All* bees would be harmed by the chemical sprays.

To test the importance of bees, farmers placed cages over their orchard trees. The cages kept bees from fertilizing the trees' blossoms. The result was that only 1 percent of the blooms produced fruit. When the bees were allowed to fertilize the trees, that figure rose to 44 percent.

When a bee visits a flower to collect honey or pollen, small grains of pollen stick to its hairy legs. As the bee moves from flower to flower, it automatically transfers this pollen from one plant to the next. In this way, the bee fertilizes the plants, enabling them to reproduce.

The scout's dance tells the other bees where to find a particular flower.

Bee experts have even been able to make bees more helpful in fertilizing more of one type of plant than another. The experts know that a few "scout" bees fly out to a particular type of flower first. The other bees stay back and watch for the scout's dance. Then they follow the scent of the scout's body and move to the flowers the scout points out. Beekeepers can now train bees to pick up a particular flower scent and move to flowers with that same scent.

If bees are first fed a sugar solution scented with the fragrance of a particular flower, they will automatically seek out that scent when searching for food in the fields.

The world cannot get along without the helpful bees. But what about the Africanized killer bees? These insects leave destruction and death in their paths. Their numbers are growing. The killer bees are on the move northward. Is there any way to stop them?

Chapter 6

SMUGGLERS AND STOWAWAYS

What would happen if an Africanized killer bee came to the United States? Worse yet, what if one is already here? A beekeeper interested in increasing his honey production could easily smuggle one in. In fact, United States authorities fear that there is a great temptation to bring killer bees across the border.

In Mexico, for example, honey production is an important part of the country's economy. Many of Mexico's beekeepers think that the

Africanized bees' killer instinct isn't that bad. "We'd get a nice harvest from them," said the Mexican owner of the largest honey production plant in the world. Such greed may very well threaten human survival. For the time being, these killer bees are kept in controlled hives.

Keeping the bees out of the United States is the job of the Animal and Plant Health Inspection Service. It's not an easy task. At John F. Kennedy International Airport in New York, almost half a million people arrive each month. Any one of them could smuggle in a killer queen bee. The risk becomes even greater when you realize that thousands of people also enter the United States through other airports all around the country.

The bees might even arrive in the United States by accident. They might be stowaways on passenger and cargo ships. In the past five years alone, inspectors have discovered dozens of beehives hidden under or between the wooden beams of many ships entering United States ports. Of course, these are the nice, normal hives of nice, normal bees. *Or are they?*

How can inspectors tell an Africanized bee from an ordinary bee? The answer is simple.

They can't. The two breeds look exactly the same. For now, any bee found on an incoming ship is considered to be a killer bee. Researchers are trying to find ways to identify the ones that came from Africa. But their work is conducted in laboratories, far away from the ships that arrive each day. It may be a long time before the researchers' work is of any help.

Many scientists and beekeepers fear that if the bees reach the United States, there could be disastrous results. Bee stings, they explain, already claim more lives than shark, snake, and spider bites combined. What would happen if *killer* bees arrived? There's just no way to predict the outcome. All we can say is it would be *bad—very bad!*

Beekeepers would have problems, too. Since Africanized bees tend to swarm more frequently than other bee species, they are more difficult to control. Beekeepers who truck hives from farm to farm would find it harder to keep these killer bees in captivity. And even if they could control and handle them, the beekeepers themselves would be in constant danger of attack from the very insects who work for them.

After these bees have finished stinging the man's arm, they will die. The bee cannot pull the stinger out without tearing away a part of its own body.

Chapter 7

CAN WE STOP THEM?

It is now 10 years since 26 African bees escaped from Dr. Kerr's labs in Brazil. Today, 90 percent of the new bees born in South America are the killer breed. Just ten years and the killer bees already outnumber all others in Brazil. Their movement to other parts of South America has been slow and steady. North of Brazil, reports of the killer bee are increasing rapidly.

For the first time, killer bee hives have been discovered under the tile roofs of houses in

A wild bee colony made this honeycomb in a
rotten beech tree.

South American cities, on statues in town
squares, and in abandoned buildings. The killer
bees are moving ever closer to human beings

and animals. Are there killer bees alive inside every hive? No one waits to find out!

In towns and villages all over South America, fire departments have organized specially trained *bee squads*. Their job is to inspect suspicious-looking hives—and kill the bees. Once the bees are dead, the firemen scoop out the honeycomb and destroy the eggs. In Recife, a town in northern Brazil, the bee squad averages four calls a day. In Aracuju, a similar team

These wild South American bees are being put into a box after landing in a new town. Killer bees rarely sting when moving into a new home.

reports as many as 20 calls a day during the swarming season.

Some towns have also organized bee cooperatives to help the citizens learn how to protect themselves against the bees. The cooperatives also teach beekeepers how to remove the more aggressive bees, even though they produce more honey.

Because the bees keep moving, stopping them has become an international problem. In Brazil, Dr. Kerr and other scientists are continuing their work. They hope to learn more about the killer bees' habits. They constantly watch the bees' movements, trying to determine if and when they'll reach points farther north.

Dr. Kerr still believes strongly that the answer to the killer bee problem lies in genetics. He believes that the killer strain can be removed by careful cross-breeding. Although it was cross-mating that caused this problem in the first place, he feels it will also save the day. So he continues to try different mating combinations, hoping that he will find a way to calm the killer bees. Of course, based on past experiences, many other scientists think Kerr will fail. They believe nothing will now stop the flight of the killer bee.

Scientists in Louisiana are also experimenting with breeding remedies. At the Bioenvironmental Bee Laboratory, researchers are examining bees from Africa and South America. They are trying to find out what other kinds of insects or parasites might be used as an "army" to control an invasion by the killer bees. Finally, bee experts are trying to find new ways of identifying the killer bee from its European cousin. If the killer bee can be spotted, it may be we can find a way to destroy it, leaving the normal bees free to do their valuable work.

Based on the distances they move—200 miles a year—scientists estimate that the killer bees will reach Panama in 6 years. If they can cross the Panama Canal, it will be clear flying into Mexico. (At present, only a few honey-producing hives have killer bees.) That would mean that killer bees could reach the southern United States by the 1990s. *The very thought is chilling!*

Can they cross the Panama Canal? Most bees don't like to cross large bodies of water. But these bees are not *most* bees. Years ago, no one thought they would cross the Amazon River. *They did.*

Will killer bees cross the Panama Canal?
Years ago, no one thought the killer bees would cross the
Amazon River. They did!

Some experts feel the bees will be stopped by cold temperatures. But killer bees have shown they can adapt to all conditions. Who's to say they can't get used to colder climates, too? Besides, the greatest swarming activity occurs in spring and fall, a time when the southern states are extremely warm.

The logical place to stop the bees is the Isthmus of Panama—a narrow strip of land connecting South America to Central America. Some scientists believe that a "breeding barrier" could be effective. As the killer bees close in on this area, the scientists would let loose great numbers of a completely new species of bee. The new bee would be bred to be stronger but gentler than the killers. Stronger, gentler male bees would mate with killer queens to produce new generations of less aggressive bees.

Other scientists don't think this plan will work. There's always the chance that another "breeding accident" might happen. It's even possible that the new bee would be *more* vicious than the Africanized bee.

Another idea would be to let loose the natural enemies of the bee. One possibility is the

Trupanwa apivora, the "bee killer." This fly can capture honeybees in flight. One such fly has been known to kill 141 bees in a single day. A drawback to this kind of plan is that flooding an area with a new insect might also disturb na-

As bees have natural enemies, so do spiders. This spider is being paralyzed by a Blue-Mud Dauber Wasp.

ture's balance. Normal, helpful insects would be destroyed in large numbers.

Other ideas for stopping the bees in Central America include luring them into poisoned beehives. Some people even suggested rigging up a high net across the Panama Canal Zone!

The facts seem to be frightening. But some United States experts believe there really isn't a problem at all. They say the bees aren't a threat to the United States. Generations of bees will have been born by the time the killer bees reach United States shores. By then, frequent interbreeding with gentler bees will have calmed down their vicious behavior.

That's already happened in the cooler, southern parts of South America. Scientists can only guess why. Perhaps it's because the wilder strains have been killed off. Or maybe the Africanized bee has interbred more frequently in the southern regions. Possibly, the new bees aren't as wild in the cooler climates.

In this mystery, there are still no real answers—and *answers are needed* to avoid

Face to face with the "killer."

further tragedy and death. Nevertheless, beekeepers in the southern parts of South America
now praise the same insect they feared a few
years ago. Because they are now better able to
handle the killer bees, the increased honey pro-

duction seems to make up for the bees' stings. But does it?

As a result of the new bee, honey production is on the rise in Brazil. And, after all, that's all that anyone could have hoped for when Dr. Kerr's project first began. Of course, there are now many Brazilians who have paid a high price for all the new honey. It cost them their *lives!* What will the killer bees finally cost the world?